HABITS OF DESERT ANIMALS

DESERT ANIMALS

Lynn M. Stone

Rourke Publications, Inc.
Vero Beach, Florida 32964

Edited by Pamela J.P. Schroeder

PHOTO CREDITS
Photos pages 7, 8, 12 © Joe McDonald; all other photos
© Lynn M. Stone

ACKNOWLEDGEMENT
The author thanks the staff of the Arizona-Sonora Desert Museum,
Tucson, for its cooperation with some of the photography in
this book.

Library of Congress Cataloging-in-Publication Data
Stone, Lynn M.
    Habits of desert animals / by Lynn Stone.
        p.   cm. — (Desert animals)
    Summary: Describes the behavior and daily lives of various
desert animals, including the jack rabbit, cactus wren, and
rattlesnake.
    ISBN 0-86625-627-X
    1. Animal behavior—Juvenile literature. 2. Desert animals—
Juvenile literature. [1. Desert animals.]   I. Title.
II. Series: Stone, Lynn M.   Desert animals.
QL751.5.S77   1997
591.754—dc21   97-16380
                                                   CIP
                                                   AC

Printed in the USA

TABLE OF CONTENTS

HABITS OF DESERT ANIMALS

The deserts of America's West and Southwest are dry, windy lands. Water is scarce. Summers are oven hot. Winters are cool, or even cold. There are few plants. Many of these are dry or thorny.

Even in such a harsh land, animals have found ways to live in the desert. The things they do and how they do them—their **habits** (HAH bits)—help them survive in amazing ways.

Habits aren't things that animals think about. They are **instinctive** (in STINK tihv), things animals do by nature's design.

The banded snake is the most skilled of the desert's "sand swimming" snakes. It slips through loose sand so easily it seems to swim.

HIBERNATING

The habit of some desert animals is to **hibernate** (HI ber nayt) each winter. Hibernation is a deep winter sleep. An animal's body systems, such as its heart rate, slow down.

Animals in the desert hibernate because there is little food in cold months. Cold weather is also a reason to hibernate. For example, it's hard for lizards and snakes to move when they're cold.

Along with lizards and snakes, bats, ground squirrels, and many insects hibernate.

The wood rat is active at night during warm weather. This rodent avoids winter and hibernates until spring.

POLLINATING

Some bats and birds of the desert sip nectar. Nectar is a sweet liquid in flowers.

Bats sip nectar by dipping their snouts into flower blossoms. Hummingbirds use their bills. While sipping the nectar, these animals also brush against flower pollen. Pollen looks like specks of yellow dust.

By flying from plant to plant, bats and hummingbirds become **pollinators** (PAH lih nay terz). They leave pollen from one blossom on another.

That transfer of pollen is important to plants. It helps them make new plants.

By sipping nectar, hummingbirds take pollen from one desert plant to another. That helps plants to grow new plants.

TRAVELING

Full-time life in the desert isn't nature's plan for most animals. Many birds visit the desert for only a few days or weeks. Birds can fly. That makes travel into and away from the desert easy.

Many birds visit the desert in spring, when it's green and cool. When summer comes and the sun bakes the desert, many **species** (SPEE sheez), or kinds, of birds **migrate** (MY grate) to cooler places.

Some bats migrate from cold to warmer deserts each fall. In spring, like many birds, they return to more northern deserts.

Like many desert birds, the hooded oriole leaves cool, northern deserts to winter in warmer, southern places.

With long, powerful hind legs, the black-tailed jackrabbit is built for flight—
on land, of course.

Camouflaged on desert pebbles, the horned lizard blends beautifully with its surroundings.

RUNNING

Running fast keeps many desert animals alive. Even a few reptiles depend on speed. The little zebra lizard, for example, can run 18 miles (29 kilometers) per hour!

Jackrabbits use speed to escape coyotes. Coyotes need speed, too, to catch jackrabbits.

The rare desert pronghorn is the fastest desert animal. Pronghorns can race at 60 miles (97 km) per hour.

Ready to run, the zebra lizard depends upon speed to keep a step ahead of bigger predators.

HOME BUILDING

Animal homes may be shelters or nests for young. Most of the desert's home builders, except for burrowers, are birds.

The cactus wren builds one of the fanciest nests. It's a large, baglike nest woven with grass, twigs, and flower stems.

The hooded oriole builds a basket nest. Costa's hummingbird makes a cuplike nest held together with spider webs.

The wood rat makes a big dome home of twigs and bits of anything it can pack.

A careful cactus wren weaves its nest among sharp spines of cholla cactus.

HUNTING

Hunting is the way that desert **predators** (PRED uh torz) survive. One of the most feared hunters is the rattlesnake.

Many species of rattlers live in American deserts. With a bite, the rattler pumps venom, or poison, through hollow fangs. Rattlers' favorite prey are rodents or rabbits.

The rattler, after striking, lets the struggling prey go. The snake doesn't want a broken tooth.

The wounded victim wanders off. However, the rattler has an amazing sense organ that tracks the victim's heat trail. The heat trail leads the snake to its prey.

This tiger rattlesnake's tongue "tests" the air to find prey. Rattlesnakes don't see well, but they sense heat and location very well.

HIDING

Some animals hide to survive. These are creatures whose fur, feathers, or scales look like their surroundings. It means they can hide, nest, or hunt with little chance of being seen by predators or prey.

The rattler, for example, can hunt from ambush because it's so hard to see. No animal, though, has better **camouflage** (KA muh flahj) than the horned lizard. This ant-eating reptile hides from big predators easily. Its scaly skin is a perfect match for the soil.

Glossary

camouflage (KA muh flahj) — hiding by blending in with the surroundings

habit (HAH bit) — the actions that make up an animal's behavior; something an animal does naturally, such as eating

hibernate (HI ber nayt) — to enter the deep, sleeplike condition in which some animals spend the winter

instinctive (in STINK tihv) — activities an animal does without thinking

migrate (MY grate) — to make a long journey at the same time and to the same place each year

pollinator (PAH lih nay ter) — an animal that takes pollen grains from one plant to another

predator (PRED uh tor) — an animal that kills other animals for food

species (SPEE sheez) — a certain kind of animal within a closely-related group of animals; for example, a *tiger* rattlesnake

INDEX